Hearing the Underwater

poems by

Savannah Slone

Finishing Line Press
Georgetown, Kentucky

Hearing the Underwater

ACKNOWLEDGMENTS

I want to thank the publishing staff, editors, and design team at *Finishing Line
Press* for believing in my work. Thank you to my fellow writers who spent time and
offered feedback, as the pieces within this collection came to be. Your thoughts mean
everything to me and I couldn't be more appreciative of your role in my revision
process. The gratitude and unconditional love I have for my family and friends
who have supported me in my writing endeavors is boundless; thank you for your
empowering encouragement. To the forests, mountains, rivers, and general magic of
the small Pacific Northwest town that I am fortunate enough to call home and draw
inspiration from, I thank you. I am equally grateful to the editors of the following
journals who previously published poems from this manuscript.

Boston Accent Lit: "Defund the Female Phobic"

Creative Colloquy: "Forewarning Pantoum"

Heavy Feather Review: "slice"

Manastash Literary Arts Magazine: "hollow lungs, eyes, kazoos, and fingernails";
"Because You Asked About Love, I'll Tell You"

The Airgonaut: "Ode to the Uterus"; "Conflict, Changing Lanes, and the Hypocritical
Silence that Ensues"; "Within Your White Picket Fence"

Publisher: Leah Maines
Editor: Christen Kincaid
Cover Art: M. Nixon of *Marz Art,* http://www.themarzart.wordpress.com
Author Photo: Tegan Shelton
Cover Design: M. Nixon of *Marz Art,* http://www.themarzart.wordpress.com

Printed in the USA on acid-free paper.
Order online: www.finishinglinepress.com
also available on amazon.com

Author inquiries and mail orders:
Finishing Line Press
P. O. Box 1626
Georgetown, Kentucky 40324
U. S. A.

Table of Contents

–for all of the selves I've been and will be

Venal Exodus

Chalkboard paint. Bruises.
The Midnight Cousin
Hallway Attack "horsing around"
kind of bruises. Cigarette exhalation wafts

seep into pores. Three sizzling ticks, pulled
loose from juvenile, hairless armpits.
Chewing tobacco forearm
application: bee stinger

liberation. Water sprinklers the only
drink the hay for grass will be seeing.
Butt burnt by rooftop sun glare.
Warm wind blows book

pages the wrong direction.
I give up.
I go in.
Two swift snaps. Caught

"playing sex" in Grandma's Powder Room.
Eyes that pierce, perforate. *Snap. Snap.*
The slow-motion heart
beat as we can't do anything

and the police don't do anything
and then one curt shotgun blast
heard through the phone. *Bang.*
Mom's boyfriend stains field

crimson with self-inflicted farewell.
Phone drops, hovers. Cord bounces it
as it levitates in limbo. Humming shrieks
ooze from levitating phone. Now:

fall face first into the couch. Real
sex in Grandma's Powder Room. Fast,

fast forward. Child drives, child
graduates high school, child

births child. Child takes child
to school. Innocence drowned.
Innocence envied. Chalk screeches
stiff line. Bruises fade. Cigarettes

tamped into ash. Armpits sliced
by shaking shaver. *Snap. Snap. Bang.*
Are you still crying because he did this to your family
or are you just mad that now you won't ever

get to take
this
option
out?

Cynicism and Other Synonyms

When I have greasy hair,
I am incapable of being happy,
yet I put it off just long enough
because feeling agitated feels good
     sometimes.

I take off my black lace bra
That I wear with my red underwear that don't match.
My bra that holds my breasts that don't match
They fed a baby who can, now, feed himself
And now, all I can do is feed myself.

Overheated
in the steam of the late-night shower,
I can feel everything
     more.

My heart beat
in my hands, blood pumping to my skull,
unnerves me. The cheap wooden
analog clock
that needs it's batteries
changed more often than it ought to
hums to me—
rocks me in its arms
of my false reality that
     I need.

It's 1 a.m.
and I'm writing without being told to
and it feels dirty,
even though it's what I'm supposed to do.
I should wipe off the post-shower mirror fog,
but I don't need to see
what I look like to see
     what I look like.

Moths try
to enter through a dark
window. They see my light
and they want in, but I don't
want anymore holes
in my clothes
or my life.

Sometimes, when I'm in the shower,
a spider will be crawling
toward me on the wet white tile wall
and I'll be stuck
in two realms:
unfounded fear
and awestruck observation.
That's how I feel most of the time, really.

And sometimes when
people talk to me, they'll
be talking about nothing
and all I'll hear is Mozart's
Requiem in D minor and I'm
not really
          there. And I'm not really here.

I have dreams of a grey house with
blue walls and a blue sofa and blue books that I have
on display, to reiterate that I read. *I'm very cool, by the way.*

Yet, I look at her and I see
me and I see hope and a future
and other clichés about love that I didn't
think were real or at least couldn't be real
for Me (n.): damaged hermit.

So maybe, just maybe, it might

be time to dissociate myself
and my name
with cynicism
and other synonyms
because
  here I am,

      here.

slice

Now is the time to
grab your eggshell paint
Pray that you won't get it in your eyes
when you stroke it across your

face. Your face that has seen
Your face that ought not be seen
If it gets in your eyes, you
might miss the removal of a hijab

Two men kissing in shame
White pointed hats
White emergency room ceilings
after a back alley abortion

Towers that gleam
and scheme
the American dream.
Pray, but only to our country's
leader: our one and only Lord,
Jesus Christ

Slice your native tongue off
and stuff it into the leg of your suit
or stitch your mouth shut with a needle and thread Know that this was
    an excellent business decision

or you could always
revolt
against the United States
of Hate
and Privilege.

Ode To The Uterus

endometrium vessel lives in the ovum office of my temple of starlight fingernails that type out plum promises of your magical expiration date, late. redemption dahlias in other muscular dimensions release thick honey apologies, pulse pleas through muting period panties pemetrium pelvic power, yeah, hollow womb. slam your legs shut so they echo through the gymnasium of assholes who just saw your crimson crotched shorts. shoreline mirrors sex mirrors making me a mother mirrors making my mother's mother's mother a mother. liners of lining leak sporadic spells of searing shedding stain my sea of sheets. climactic whispers brood and bleed, they whisper whispers of their reproductive rights to contraception, yeah, you moan cries of regulation through menstruation. myometrium fertilized fetal petal, short goodbyes through constellations of toilet trickles.

Conflict, Changing Lanes, and the Hypocritical Silence that Ensues

The fear of coughing in class at another new high school. The new girl. Eyes, slow dripping faucets. Her scratchy, shaking esophagus wants to whisper, *Don't breathe. Don't breathe.* But can't. She can tell you about the fear of crossing the road because what if the person in that car 100 feet away thinks she's annoying for not letting them go first. Peach tinted birth control pills sometimes go forgotten since she stopped sleeping with men. When she and her mom are in the kitchen at the same time, since she's an adult who still lives at home, the mom says something like, "You know that lesbian sex can't get you pregnant, right?" But she has acne and endometriosis and did you know that her baby sucked the life out of her breasts? The baby favored the left one. Three years later, you can still tell that the baby favored the left one. Did you know that what she's really thinking about, during sad parts in movies, is about the camera crew and the call of "cut" so she doesn't show any weakness? Incessant apologies. Incessant cold sweats. In constant need of compression and chiropractic care with the anxiety that lingers and cripples and tells her she's not like everybody else. She's the girl you don't want to start a story with that you can't finish right now. Who conflict disarms. Who won't tell you no. Who won't do anything if you don't hear "no". She's the girl who justifies herself with phrases like, "I don't like conflict." Who won't stand for injustice, unless it is her own. She's the girl who tells everyone else to not be who she secretly is, on the inside. They leave, empowered, and then she sits in her own hypocritical silence. Sitting across from her therapist, she follows up every childhood tragedy with a laugh that might as well be paired with finger guns. The therapist looks concerned. "Would you say you use humor as a coping mechanism?" The fear of changing lanes on the highway. The fear of being shot in a school. In a movie theatre. In a mall. At a concert. *But she doesn't go to concerts.* In a church. *No, she doesn't go to church, either.* She doesn't remember the date of conception of concealing herself. She will tell you about her everyday life, sure, but will she tell you about that hour of the night when the most nightmarish of scenarios seem conceivable? No, she won't. She'll tell you about the books she'd recommend and the funny thing her son said last week and her five year plan and the story she's writing that she's very barely writing and the expected snow and how she fears her commute in that expected snow and, and, and...

magic, blue lights, and velvet loveseats

missed peripheral grasps
kick me in the stomach. I can feel
my own palm as if it weren't my
own. like rubbing cream colored
silk against cream colored silk.
foreign slow motion
walking meditations with you, all in my head.
your northern lights firefly eyes glow
a surgeon's glove blue.
Resuscitation.
deep breaths feel like orgasms
when I'm drunk on perception.
slow pedestrians
slow clap
and we move slowly, too.

Defund the Female Phobic

We advocate for accessibility.
You support life until first breath.
You support life until that life needs support.
We just said no to abstinence.
Our selection was contraception, but regulation trumps
reproductive rights. You ejaculate hate,
defunding our consenting cervixes and
their intra-uterine devices and
their human papilloma viruses.
Morning after pills are needed for this orgasmic
oppression. Impede the silencing
intolerance from the female phobic.

A (Self) Love Story

I'm going to tell you a truth and a lie: I love myself. Hearing myself talk. Preaching but not following my own "How-To" manifesto. How to be confident, despite your physical flaws, in the eyes, the penetrating eyes, of the condemnatory seventh grade classroom. How to not let stigma around mental illness define your own. How to come to terms with your trauma. *It's not your fault. Don't blame yourself.* I thrive on compliments of my mind. I value myself, my separate self. My physical self a reminder that I hate myself for hating myself. *Body-positivity* until my own body is involved in the conversation. *Everyone is beautiful* until a compliment comes my way. My soul, self-contradicting, apprehensive. Never making my days' ends plausible. Assumptions of outside judgments, irrational thoughts mirror back. I wade in the shallow end of my misunderstandings of self vs. the world. Repetitive acts of self-loathing drive, my separate successor prospers. I give, don't follow. Shadowing behind what I don't have to offer into an underwater depth of clandestine dejection. I can tell you that I love myself and it's true, but my many masks mystify. Sometimes revulsion defeats and I'm left alone, parched, while my mouth and lungs are filled to the brim with waves, spitting out the overflow, trying to fight for myself.

Within Your White Picket Fence

sits a large, locked house
a tightly shut, white
trimmed window has no eyes
that peer out and no eyes
peering in
in front of your T.V. sits your white
husband and his white wife
you're shocked you're both shocked
you pray
your robotic exoskeletons
move through the motions
you both send love and you pray
your prayers nuclear
your prayers can even stop mass shootings
you have your paper towels
you even have spare rolls
your erasure tongues don't
decompose your rags don't fill the dying bullet
holes of those whose throats are running raw
screaming spewing trapped
throats in constellations of smoke with window
seats into loopholes
now is not the time to talk
about the why, no, now is the time to pray
pause now is the time to pray again
it has happened again and
pause it has happened again
let's not point fingers let's dance
eyes sewn shut as the automatic
hum vibrates the ground
we pray on as the mounds of orphaned
pleas and rising statistics
pause it has happened
again

The Underwater

It's the morning
light that glows
through my beige
book page.

The slow motion
wind funnel that swirls
foliage and
the grocery sack in *American Beauty.*

A single glance that
friends just don't share. Skepticism
and solitary morph with that
glimpse. The embrace of tree
tunnel leaves make me
not want to leave,
for once.

The relief of the tunnel,
when I, windshield wipers, fight
for my life
through the hammering rain.

I squeal dry until I have to
reenter the world, on my own. Makes me
gasp for breath, knowing how long
I had been here, but hadn't
yet been born. It's red velvet Mary Jane's skipping down the
saturated street.

Chipped sea foam paint and chipped black
nail polish. Magnetic poetry and the hum
of the underwater. Hollow lunged mermaids
drawn home to the underwater.

hollow lungs, eyes, kazoos, and fingernails

We bury disassembled
rag dolls, pouring the nectar of humanity
over top the neglected
handcuffs.
Our mystical wild
eyes flutter
among the discarded
crayons. We see the dark-eyed,
deafening earth
swallow the cheap feathers—
drawn down in the black glass,
among hazy
footprints of blood.
These faceless footprints
render our shattered
tongues outnumbered.
Our crooked mouths duct
taped. Our jaws gripped
by the vibrating
fingernails of our nemesis.
We see the delicate peach pits
in the urns of your overall
pockets. We hear your
shadow. The watercolor
humming of the bees
and their kazoos make us swallow
the florescent Morse code rot
of our minds' inner workings. Inky cigarette
ashes shiver
beneath the graffiti
rot while conceptualized universes
dance in the machine shadows.
You discard empty
prayers of empty generosity.
They shimmer from your gold,
hollow lungs.

Because You Asked About Love, I'll Tell You

Love should be
heard: an unannounced
gasp—the flicking
of a lighter
the cracking
of knuckles
a deep inhalation
as a breeze
envelops your
body.

should be
felt: the full body
cringe when the untimely,
wandering deer inhales
a concluding breath—like chilled,
aching breaths
during a frosty
jog like the
first
thrust of your
first.

should be
unanticipated—
should make you
reconsider
every thought
every theory
leading up to
the moment your
fingertips graze that
sacred page.

should be
a blind trudge
through thick

soil in search
of yourself—
your voice.

should be
finding home
in sketchy alleys
with flickering,
shot at, shattered glass
streetlamps and quaint
cafes where the era
of the smoking section
lingers upon the wallpaper's
yellow tinted rosebuds
and rundown hotel rooms
and their sheets that tell stories.

A love should be
should be
should be

roots

Calendars dissolve,
reminding me of
lifeless, wasted breath.
White wall clocks beat their
simulated ticks.
Confined: to endure?
Wandering, though there's
nothing to perceive.
Confused journal logs
attempt to make sense.
Many-a-time, I
erased and rewrote.
Erased and rewrote.
I crave meaning from
This weary world where
I live and will leave.
I rewrite to see.
I turn the doorknob,
to dig for my roots.

Erasure Poem from Virginia Woolf's "The Voyage Out"

The **sparkle** **of dissipation** **was unusually dull** **which** **prompted** **silence** **to** **a** **conversation** **of** **mind**

Cycle Demise

Inner child
hears the nice white
lady with her nice
inverted bob who squeaks
out the inevitable, "What are you
going to be when you
grow up?" A bee might tickle

your thigh, meandering through its limited
time. Consider the impossibility
of stillness, as you flirt
with the icicle you
lay beneath. "Same as you," you
respond, to her surprise. Listen to the synchronized
steps of pedestrians that thump

the ground: an earthquake
of human noise. "Oh, you want to work in insurance?"
Her head will twist
like a perplexed dog. Her bob
will meld, asymmetrical. Moving at last.
She won't want to hear the truth, but you're a child—
you don't know any better. Go ahead now, darling. Shock her.

"No.
Dead."
Her false smile will tighten
into a very particular "o".
You just might catch a glimpse
into the real being underneath
if you look through that window

closely enough. She doesn't understand
why a child would be so morbid. Admire the bubbles
that slip from your lips' airtight seal,
dancing to the crack of your back
in the claw foot bathtub. Your spine emits

the tinny piano song of your life thus far. Mouth pressed
tight, eyes pressed tight, the outside a hum

that doesn't matter. "You're going to die and so am I,
so what does it matter what my corpse does
in the mean time?" She stills. Passersby still.
Their halted heels falter, standing on the bleeding

bodies of the silenced. They apply their headphones
and walk on. Footsteps impale. The nice white
lady pats her leg for you to follow, but you lay down

in your fellow human's cherry pool
of demise instead. The heels dig in,
ending it before it can begin.
Warm hand interlaced
with cold hand.
Hatred expires.
Cadavers indistinguishable.

280 days in

bathtub with plastic for walls filled to maximum capacity
with cloudy water, epsom salt, and tears. mother's hug
a muted lecture. ears are deafened by her thick, mole ridden
shoulder. she leaves the bathroom. a dollar tree receipt and a
puddle of urine sit under a plastic clump of ill timing. he left.
they all leave. mirror eye contact fades to blurred outlines.
you are not your own. cautious foot placements cradle
unsteady river rocks. i levitate as the breathy wind exhales
me higher. passersby toss tethers at me. pulling at my limbs,
they stretch me to beyond.

i am a calf. i am a newborn. taken from my mother
and thrown onto the ground. the passersby look down
at me. they took a good, long look. my too tight, tacky wind-
breaker scratches out a rustling hush as i walk up an asphalt
hill. a squirrel is drunk, staggering in and out of the road
in front of me. i can't breathe or talk or stand up straight,
but my heavy eyes meet his. he sees me. i walk on. i offer
my full weight to my mother, dangling around her neck
like the necklace i should have bought her for her
fiftieth birthday. i wade in the bath water and eat raspberries.

waiting, a dance of fear engulfs me. woman. they all come.
he comes. i see my eyes in his eyes. they look like mine.
we are our own.

As you've heard

I am the trunk

                    of the trees that seize

I am the breeze

                    magnetizing wind chimes

My palms grow near as iron draws near

                    to profess a clanging of

their undying love. I am The child of

                    the roots of the dahlias

the bulb

                    I am the bulb

I am your grandmother's perfume

                    Begging to be squeezed and released

I am the mermaid's seashell comb

                    I am the last sip of tea

Earthy and thick

                    I am

Self Care and Other Unattainables

You start your days motivated. Coffee. Check off lists.
Eight illustrated water droplets to remind yourself
to take care of yourself. You
look in the mirror at your acne,
now adult acne. You can't eat healthy anymore. You buy
food items like "Uncrustables" and "Spaghettios" these days
because existing feels like wading through a pool of syrup
that you can never break free from
and the last time you
were going to a therapist, you would put on
a mask and change the subject every time you
might not seem sane. You
go to Goodwill. You
buy jeans in the next few sizes up
because you know yourself.
You wade numbly, listening
to audiobooks when you're not quite up
for turning book pages and wait for the future.
The kind of future where there's time
for you. There can't be time for you
when you're checking off everyone
else's check lists, too.
You adopt this new self that cares
too much and doesn't care enough. You
tend to it with the care and patience
every parent wants to have.
You want to be this idea of a person
that you don't really know and don't
really know how to be. You end your
days motivated, again, but too tired to execute
anything serious. You thumb your unchecked
check off lists, frustrated with yourself. You
want to want to take
better care of yourself, but you're
not in the mood and neither am I.

Middle School

This is the clammy
intelligence in the sour
museum shadows of
the nights you'll never have.
This is how you Google
"Playboy" for full body
flip phone
thirteen-year-old
photograph inspiration.
This is how you scramble
back to your floral sheets
every time mom's
snoring pauses.
This is how you set up
reading lamps as the next best thing
to the professional grade lighting
that WikiHow said you'd need.
These are juvenile cum soaked
basketball shorts and these are the cracking
voices that tell you "You're hot" or,
what you hear:
"You're worthy of being here."
This is the respective erection: a crutch for collapse.
This is the prospective mold
a window to silenced heirlooms.
This is you, a prop. This is me,
a premonition.

I don't know

where I come from, Big Bang
or Adam and Eve? I don't know
if my choosing not
to drop out of school and sell
heroin *matters.*
Frequent over the shoulder
glances and crooked cash
or straight A's?
What is the difference
when we're back where we began?
I don't know
if I will see the dead again. Are they watching
over me like my Grandma
and the preacher
and the motherless child say, or
are they
simply coffin-housed corpses?
I don't know
if there is a point to all of this. I don't know
what the darkness
of nothing looked like
before there was darkness.

shot down

Ekphrastic poem in response to Frida Kahlo's "La venadita (little deer)"

Punctured
Once for flipping off the catcaller.
Second for eating too much, then too
little, then too much again.
Third for expecting the same wage
as you, for the same job.
Fourth for not covering up my flawed face.
Fifth for not going swimming on the first date.
Sixth for not submitting to my husband's every dictation.
Seventh for not being in the mood.
Eighth for asking to make my
own choices for my body.
Ninth for saying I had a boyfriend,
just so you wouldn't shoot
me in the heart with an arrow.
Rejected rejection—
Shot down for speaking my mind.

Forewarning Pantoum

Cannonading seas warn of malevolent presences.
Ominous seagull song tells stories of impending terror.
Intentions of abduction: their shadows threaten my existence.
Vile shadows inch nearer. I scramble. Safe harbor.

Ominous seagull song tells stories of impending terror.
My fearful feet wade—unwilling to run.
Vile shadows inch nearer. I scramble. Safe harbor.
My body beats a tempest of panic.

My fearful feet wade—unwilling to run.
The ocean's multiple personalities pull me this way and that.
My body beats a tempest of panic.
Last minute maternal liberation; near abduction. Rescued.

The ocean's multiple personalities pull me this way and that.
Cannonading seas warn of malevolent presences.
Last minute maternal liberation; near abduction. Rescued.
Intentions of abduction: their shadows threaten my existence.

Maternal Encounters of Disregard

Blood pressure. Heart rate. Temperature. Urine sample.
Walk in clinic, doctor-of-the-day says,
Your pregnancy test came back positive
Her eyes offer sympathy, as they look down on me.
Asymmetrical bob, alligator-shoes-wearing doctor-
of-the-day assumes abortion because
I'm seventeen and apparently incapable.
Pro-choice, but it wasn't the choice for me.
High school graduation, belly still flat. Undisclosed news.
It was kind of nice to not have anyone disappointed in me yet.
It was kind of nice to pretend
I was still going off to college
(i.e. flying the nest and other things still on my to-do list).
That isn't your baby, is it?
Clinical Psychologist's pale hands open folder
of findings. Clinical psychologist says,
Your child has autism
Ears ring. Slow blink melts
in the inexorable roundabout,
renders me seasick in the ocean's
weight: fills cathartic jars.
Are you his nanny?
            Mommy needs a minute

The Table Where We Sat and Sit

Trying to make end's meet

One Christmas, I gifted my mom an orphaned quarter that I found, because then she couldn't say, *I don't have a dime to my name* anymore. A quarter was even more than a dime. Habitually reading *The Table Where the Rich People Sit* to reassure me that we're better off.

Stealing toilet paper from the school in my *not-even-Jansport* backpack. Smelled like somebody else's mom's cigarettes. Living wherever there wasn't rent. Goodwill trips.

But I'm a single mom

Growing up poor means I now have my own money, and I can't stop spending after never having enough. Never breaking eye contact with the pickpocket's pocket. Gypsy butterflies migrating, teaching me value.

You don't want to be rich because rich people don't appreciate things.

Now, here I am, single mom, growing up poor, with my son, growing up poor. It would be so much easier to eliminate that stressor. I think I'd still appreciate things.

Muzzled Magic

First: open door. Descend porch steps. Key, ignition. Enter real world. Leave comfort of your home and hear the anthropoid clamor that never dims. Then: The melodrama of peripheral euthanasia, yarn scrapes against cracked palms. Playground of ghost tongues, hyperfixate over the hills of your body as you clang out slang and mumble grief, hungry for nostalgia and vinyl and the naked wooden montage of your moonless eyes that don't see me. My blue hair stains my shirt's shoulders in the rain, you don't stop talking. You don't stop talking about nothing. Now: exit / ignition / ascend / deadbolt / mute / recharge. / Haunting dissolutions of velvet fog treetop quilt, manifestation condolences and other forgotten, fossilized teeth. Scattered mouths pulse in the graveyard of muzzled magic

Savannah **Slone** is a queer writer who earned her B.A. in English: Professional and Creative Writing from Central Washington University and is completing her M.F.A. at Lindenwood University. Her poetry and short fiction has appeared in or will soon appear in *Heavy Feather Review, Boston Accent Lit, The Airgonaut, Ghost City Press, decomP magazinE, Maudlin House, FIVE:2:ONE, Pidgeonholes, TERSE Journal,* and elsewhere. She serves as the Assistant Poetry Editor at *Boston Accent Lit* and is a *Wigleaf* Top 50 Very Short Fictions Reader. Savannah is the mother of a child on the autism spectrum and is passionate about neurodiversity and inclusivity. Savannah's work most often pairs natural themes with examinations in mental illness, reproductive rights, sex and consent, gun control, motherhood, and what living in Trump's America looks like. She currently dwells in the Pacific Northwest with her partner and son, where she enjoys reading, knitting, hiking, and discussing intersectional feminism.

CPSIA information can be obtained
at www.ICGtesting.com
Printed in the USA
LVHW090401150119
603916LV00001B/49/P

9 781635 348217